ANTHOLOGY 2021

THE ST. JOSEPH'S ORPHANAGE RESTORATIVE INQUIRY WRITERS' GROUP

Gene Clark

Debi Gevry-Ellsworth

Sheila Grisard

Katelin Hoffman

Michael Ryan

EDITED BY

Carol Adinolfi

GReen
wriTers
press

Green Writers Press
34 Miller Road
Brattleboro, VT
www.greenwriterspress.com

CONTENTS

EDITOR'S NOTE	*Carol Adinolfi*	6
ACKNOWLEDGMENTS	*Marc Wennberg*	7
THE ST. JOSEPH'S RESTORATIVE JUSTICE INQUIRY: A BRIEF HISTORY	*Marc Wennberg & Carol Adinolfi*	8
PRAISE FOR THE WRITERS	*Christine Kenneally, Kate Brayton, & Jim Forbes*	10

ONE: WORKS IN PROGRESS, SPRING, 2020

ANTHEM	*Gene Clark*	13
EARLY MEMORIES	*Sheila Grisard*	14
RADIO OF LIFE	*Katelin Hoffman*	18
INTRODUCTION	*Gene Clark*	23
I DON'T WANT TO DO THIS		24
BETRAYED FAITH		25
IN GOD'S NAME		26
ORPHAN	*Michael Ryan*	27
THE CHILI CONTEST		29
THE THOUGHT OF YOU	*Debi Gevry-Ellsworth*	31
CROWBAR		35
THIS SISTER, THIS SNAKE		36
MYSTERY OF THE HUMAN BEING		38

PROJECTS & CONVERSATIONS

ON REVISION:
A CONVERSATION ABOUT PROCESS
Debi Gevry-Ellsworth
& Carol Adinolfi
40

THE ROCK PAINTING & INSCRIPTION
Katelin Hoffman
41

THE ROCK PROJECT:
TALKING ABOUT THE INTERPLAY
OF WRITING & VISUAL ART
Katelin Hoffman
& Carol Adinolfi
42

TOOLS FOR WRITERS & AN EXPERIMENT

THE WRITER'S NOTEBOOK
AS A TOOL
FOR GENERATING MATERIAL
Carol Adinolfi
44

AN EXPERIMENT:
MOMENTS/MEMORY FRAGMENTS
45

COLLABORATIVE CALL & RESPONSE
WRITING EXPERIMENT
46

Gene Clark

Debi Gevry-Ellsworth

Sheila Grisard

Katelin Hoffman

Michael Ryan

TWO: ONE YEAR LATER

BRICKS AND MORTAR	*Debi Gevry-Ellsworth*	50
ONCE		52
GURU TOO		54
MY SWEET ROSIE		55
A LETTER		56
SPIRITUAL EVENTS	*Gene Clark*	58
SEEMS LIKE I LIVED A LIFETIME IN MY FIRST SIX YEARS	*Katelin Hoffman*	61
FREEDOM BEHIND BARS	*Michael Ryan*	65
ABOUT THE WRITERS		68
SPECIAL THANKS		73
AN APPRECIATION		74

INTRODUCTION

*When thinking about facilitated creativity that
is focused on trauma, I see the forces of nature:
rivers and volcanoes. As traumatic memories are
brought to the surface, the experience can be
overwhelming. Individuals who have undergone
childhood abuse, in the act of remembering,
have reported sensations of drowning, of being
flooded. Through the process of creative writing
in a structured workshop setting, that intensity
and pain is channeled into an enactment of
meaning.*

— Alisa Del Tufo, Founder
Threshold Collaborative

Writing is a kind of revenge against circumstance: bad luck, loss, pain. If you make something out of it, then you've no longer been "bested" by these events.

— Louise Glück

In May of 2020, when I first met Debi Gevry-Ellsworth and asked about her hopes for the writers' group she told me she'd written poems and stories, and had kept a journal all of her life. Writing had always been a refuge but lately the blank page had become "a monster." I was immediately impressed by Debi's openness, her ability to speak honestly about intimate, important things, to a perfect stranger. Almost seamlessly, then, we shifted into collaboration mode, hammering out the announcement for the writers' workshop, doing some intensive thinking and planning. I realize now this was a microcosm of what was to come. The other members of the group would show similar candidness and vulnerability, as well as drive: to keep going, keep working, stay curious about the writing process. All of this in the midst of bringing to the surface deeply traumatic memories. The group developed quickly into a perfect model for how writers' workshops (and, in fact, all groups) should function. Camaraderie, mutual support, deep listening, generosity of spirit, and absence of criticism have all been present in our weekly gatherings, in great abundance.

While preparing for the first workshops, I'd studied Christine Kenneally's 2018 Buzzfeed article, in which she recounts the horrors inflicted upon the children of St. Joseph's.
I remember darkness and despair taking over as I read, unmitigated by the brightness of the sun, the new green of early spring in my back yard. I knew that whatever I'd learned about writing in my own education and as a teacher would be insufficient here.

I called a trusted colleague, Dawn Gilchrist. She has, throughout her career, mostly as a middle and high school English teacher, worked with students who face an immense amount of trauma in their daily lives. I asked her how I could guide the process of writing poetry and personal narratives with sensitivity. How could I ask everyone to slow down, bringing agonizing moments to life with detail? How would I talk about revision and editing in this context?

In her response, Dawn showed me how to articulate a crucial boundary, one that would insure full agency for each writer, every step of the way:

> It's important to let writers know that you find
> their story meaningful and worthwhile, and
> then, as a doorway to a secondary process,
> ask them if they want to work with it on a more
> superficial and editorial level. The idea is to have
> as many people become part of a real audience
> as possible, and the best way to do that is by
> making the writing as clear as possible and as
> clean and as precise.

Within the group's first meetings, a common theme emerged: the desire to tell the whole story. I thought back upon my own childhood, one in such contrast to the experiences of these writers. In recalling the most minor instances of unfair or unkind treatment, I noticed what was still, so many years later, a visceral response. And this helped me to understand, if only in some small way, the need to recount in detail the situation where pain has been inflicted. I tried to imagine my response, still visceral in the present, magnified by the cruelty and inhumanity of the abuses that had been inflicted upon these former children, repeatedly and over time, and I could not. There was no formula or equation by which to even remotely approach comprehension. But I recognized a universality: the intensely felt, innate sense of justice of the child.

What I could do as facilitator, I hoped, would be to encourage and show my respect for the writers and their writing at every phase, including, and especially, the words that first emerged. I could let them know that their work, whether it be spontaneous and raw or intensely revised, was important and meaningful exactly as it was. At the same time, I would present development and revision strategies for those who wanted to go further.

I don't think I ever learned to write;
I learned to revise.
— George Saunders

As the writers worked to shape their stories, I spoke of many of the same "laws" that apply to fiction writing. The writer George Saunders has said that a "perfect model" for revision is that of a conversation. In individual "revision workshops," I painted Saunders' picture of an imagined reader and the writer sitting across the table from one another. Says Saunders, "You always have a friend on the other end and if you think she's really smart and curious and worldly, it's going to be mutually interesting." With this image, these workshops became three-way conversations between writer, facilitator, and imagined reader. This "friend on the other end" grew to be a strong, neutrality-inducing presence. The idea of an audience was now more singular and palpable.

Poetry is the spontaneous overflow of
emotion… recollected in tranquility.

— William Wordsworth

If traumatic memories are a flood, then the work of structuring and shaping the work is a rope-bridge over those waters. For Debi Gevry-Ellsworth, that tranquility was hard-won, and came only after countless revisions, as she worked draft after draft to put (in the words of W.H. Auden) "the right words in the right order." It was not so much peace, perhaps, that she was looking for, but the sense of organic unity that is achieved when a poem has been "worked" (as she puts it) as far as it can be in the moment. Amongst most of the writers, a deep engagement in the revision process is somewhat new. They've begun to experience the way writing can come alive as one moves from composition to revision. I've sensed excitement in the writers as they have crafted their stories and poems. The necessary and understandable allegiance to long-held memories has been transformed. The writers are responding now to what is on the page. And, as they each have given voice and form to the trauma that lives inside the body, there is a sense of mastery in the making.

The writers' hopes for this anthology is that it will encourage others who have similar stories to tell. Through steady application over the course of a year, they have faced the blank page with fierceness, prepared to tackle difficult and painful subject matter. At St. Joseph's, they lost the freedom and innocence of childhood. But, through the process of writing this book, they have taken back, in some measure, the personal agency that was stolen from them as they were subjected to countless acts of unspeakable cruelty. As you spend some time within these pages, you will know that, against the horrendous circumstances in which they found themselves as children, these writers seem to be saying, "Let us show you with our words that we have not been bested."

EDITOR'S NOTE

"One: Works in Progress, Spring, 2020" was originally published on the St. Joseph's Orphanage Restorative Inquiry (S.J.O.R.I.) website following an online reading presented by the group to members of the S.J.O.R.I. advisory team. Along with the writers' poetry and non-fiction are several song lyrics (written prior to the workshop by Gene Clark) and craft conversations with some of the writers. In order to provide a glimpse of the workshop process, I've also included some examples of the materials we used and exercises that were helpful in generating the group's first pieces of writing.

"Two: One Year Later" is the culmination of the group's deeper dive into the revision process as well as departures from the original and central subject matter. In poetry and personal narratives, the group forayed from the direct chronicling of the orphanage experience and time span. Michael Ryan ("The Chili Contest") and Debi Gevry-Ellsworth ("Mystery of the Human Being") had been forerunners of this movement into new realms. The writers went down individual paths, following the directions in which their work was taking them. Presented here is a selection taken from a year-long process where all of life entered in. Over the year, the writers wrote of marriage, important animal companions, and lost loves, as well as experiences linked more directly to the ongoing resonations of traumas inflicted at St. Joseph's.

— Carol Adinolfi, Writer & Workshop Facilitator

ACKNOWLEDGMENTS

There isn't enough space to acknowledge all of the people and institutions who have helped make this anthology possible. We would be remiss, however, if we didn't recognize a few. First, we want to acknowledge the foundational support of the Vermont Center for Crime Victim Services, which has funded the restorative inquiry facilitation and activities. Second, we want to thank the University of Vermont Medical Center Sponsorship Fund for their generous support of the writers' group. Third, we absolutely must acknowledge the care, dedication and sheer skill of Carol Adinolfi for guiding the writers' group from its inception to the publication of this anthology. Finally, we are grateful to the anthology writers for sharing their stories with the world. Through your brave work, you hold us to rightful account, and you offer encouragement to all who may be seeking ways to creatively transform their own harms.

— Marc Wennberg, Facilitator
St. Joseph's Orphanage Restorative Inquiry

THE ST. JOSEPH'S ORPHANAGE RESTORATIVE INQUIRY: A BRIEF HISTORY

S.J.O.R.I. was launched in 2019 as a non-judicial response to the life-altering harms and abuses perpetrated at St. Joseph's Orphanage in Burlington, Vermont. The restorative inquiry's mission is to listen to, understand, and document the events of the orphanage through the voices, experiences, and stories of those most impacted (the former children) and then facilitate inclusive processes of accountability, amends-making, learning, and change.

The restorative inquiry is an initiative of the Burlington Community Justice Center and is supported by an advisory team composed of community stakeholders and restorative inquiry participants. The inquiry is informed by a set of restorative justice principles and values that guide all of our work, including our primary obligation, which is to facilitate, to the best of our abilities, the individual and collective goals of the former residents of the orphanage.

THE VOICES OF ST. JOSEPH'S

The Voices of St. Joseph's is comprised of the primary participants of the St. Joseph's Orphanage Restorative Inquiry. This group of former orphanage residents have come together to have their voices heard, seek justice as they define it, and help to end child abuse such as they experienced at the former St. Joseph's Orphanage.

Amongst their core initiatives, the group worked with Senator Chris Pearson, Senator Kesha Ram, and other Vermont legislators to pass legislation, S.99, a bill to remove removal of the Statute of Limitations for Physical Abuse. The group is also working with Burlington's Parks and Recreation Department to establish a memorial/healing space on the former orphanage property. On April 19, 2021, the group received the Vermont Center for Crime Victim Services' Survivor/Activist Award. The award is given to "the person or group that has fought through unimaginable odds and turned a personal struggle into systematic change to benefit crime victims." On this day, Marc Wennberg, facilitator of S.J.O.R.I., was also honored with the center's Crime Victim Services Ally Award.

THE S.J.O.R.I. WRITERS' GROUP

The writers' group was the inspiration of one the members of The Voices of St. Joseph's, Debi Gevry-Ellsworth. In response to the group's request to participate in an ongoing writers' workshop, S.J.O.R.I. brought in poet and creative writing instructor Carol Adinolfi to facilitate. The group has been meeting weekly since June of 2020. In addition to publishing writings from the first several months of the workshop on the S.J.O.R.I. website, the group has given several online readings. In attendance, amongst others, have been Lieutenant Governor Molly Gray and members of the Vermont Legislature.

— Marc Wennberg & Carol Adinolfi

PRAISE FOR THE WRITERS

"The writers' group has been an amazing opportunity for The Voices of St. Joseph's. Trauma is an experience of mind, body and soul. Writing, as a collective experience, is one of the most valuable tools for survivors, one that helps them to reflect upon their experiences with new eyes, and to access memories that might otherwise have remained buried. These writers have engaged fully in this therapeutic activity. With courage and strength, they have chosen to share their work with others in order to create change and engender understanding." (Kate Brayton, LICSW, Victim Services Director, Vermont State Police, Major Crime Unit)

"Reading the stories of those who lived at St. Joseph's Orphanage allowed my heart and mind to exist for a moment with them as children in that place. To witness. To stand with. We need to hear these stories, as their telling is a gift, a burden, and a challenge to us to remember with them that which should not ever occur again. My thanks for their sharing." (Jim Forbes, MPA, LICSW, Burlington, Vermont)

"The ordeal of children who spent time at St. Joseph's Orphanage in Burlington, Vermont, is one of the 20th century's darkest and least told tales. It is also one of that era's most extraordinary stories of resilience and survival. Like children in a fairy tale, the survivors of St. Joseph were locked away in a dark fortress with often cruel and abusive adults standing between them and the rest of the world. Somehow through this, the writers of this book held on to the unique spark inside them. It may have taken time to understand the fallout of their time in an orphanage, but with immense strength, courage and creativity, they came together to support each other and tell their story in their own words. Everyone who cares about history and truth should read this book. (Christine Kenneally, prize-winning journalist and author of the 2018 Buzzfeed article "We Saw Nuns Kill Children: The Ghosts of St. Joseph's Catholic Orphanage")

ONE: WORKS IN PROGRESS, SPRING, 2020

After great pain, a formal feeling comes – (372)

After great pain, a formal feeling comes –
The Nerves sit ceremonious, like Tombs –
The stiff Heart questions 'was it He, that bore,'
And 'Yesterday, or Centuries before'?

— Emily Dickinson

I want to remember my childhood, but how do I start?

*It was so long ago, so far in the past.
I remember swinging so I take my pen and write about how I felt swinging. Suddenly, more comes to me. My mother was there, then gone. My sister held my hand as we ran to the swing. I had my new shoes on. The ride to St. Joseph's, my father, my siblings, catching frogs to eat, playing in the haystack, chasing bulls. I continue to write and with all my excitement about my memories I can't write fast enough. It is so powerful to remember it all by writing it down. It isn't long before I've written 20 pages!*

— Sheila Grisard

Gene Clark

ANTHEM

We are the Children of St Joseph's.
We need our voices to be heard.
Will you hear all our truths
And take us at our word?

You didn't believe us then,
So please believe us now.
For we'll tell you all our truths
If you'll just believe somehow.

Your disbelief in us has added to our tears.
For we've lived with all these truths
For oh so many years.

We are the Children of St. Joseph's
We need our voices to be heard.
Will you hear all our truths
And take us at our word?

So, we're going to raise our voices
For everyone to hear, in spite of all your doubts
In spite of all our fears.
So please believe us now, for our pain is so sincere.
For we've lived with all this pain
For oh so many years.

Sheila Grisard

EARLY MEMORIES

In 1962, I was placed at St. Joseph's Orphanage in Burlington, Vermont. My mother, at 29, was a barmaid, and my father, at 43, was the hired help at a dairy farm. Together, they did their best to care for their nine children: six boys and three girls. We were all about one year apart in age. We lived in the main farmhouse. Dad worked hard on the dairy farm. Mom was gone most of the time working in the local town bar. There was a sugar shack on the farm, and during sugar season, Dad would tap the maple trees. I can still see him, smiling, carrying the buckets on a yoke across his shoulders. He would let us take a cup of the syrup. We'd boil it down and pour it over fresh snow for a treat.

My brothers and sisters were always around. We'd play hide-and-seek in the haystacks and tease the bull until it chased us to the safety of our big front porch. We lived in front of the railroad tracks. We'd put our ears to the track to listen for the rumble and to feel the vibration of an oncoming train. As it got closer, we'd place pennies on the track and watch the train flatten them. My sister Cheryl, who was one year older than me, would drop a sheet down a hole through the second story floor, where a stove pipe had once been. She'd tie the sheet to the bed and throw it down the pipe hole and we'd slide down the sheet and land on the floor. Raspberry picking with my dad was my favorite event. As we crossed the trestle, I felt safe riding on his foot clutching onto his leg so that I wouldn't fall through the cracks into the muddy waters below. We'd bring big buckets that had once held peanut butter; we'd fill them with plump, juicy raspberries.

I don't remember any fighting, shouting, or bad feelings with my brothers and sisters. At night, we were never tucked in. Instead, we all jumped into one big bed wearing the same clothes we'd worn all day.

My sister Linda stopped attending school at 13 so that she could stay home to care for us. She'd help us catch frogs by the pond. In the evening, she would prepare delicious frogs' legs, cook beans in a big pot, and serve those along with our favorite snack: bread with butter and sugar.

We were free to roam the countryside that surrounded the farm. Often, we would visit an elderly man who lived in a little shack down the road. He had severe scoliosis, which caused his spine to curve to the side. He limped, using a cane, and moved awkwardly about in his tiny space. He would take advantage of my older sister and myself. He bribed us with food. We took turns watching out the window for anyone who might come near. I had the sense that this was wrong. But I never knew who to tell.

Our house was quarantined once, during a scarlet fever outbreak. My brother Douglas was very red and sick. Local farmers and town folk brought us groceries and left them outside the door. My oldest brother, Tommy, 14 at the time, was considered mature enough to care for himself. So, many nights, he'd stay with friends from school. Sometimes he'd wait all night in mom's car so he could drive her home from the bar.

I remember a day in late fall, just after my brother Lonny was born. Three families were having their ninth child in close proximity, and the order of sequence was exactly the same in each family.

A local reporter thought this would make an interesting story. For the momentous occasion of his visit to our home, my sister and I had our waist-long hair cut to chin length.

My brothers all had their hair neatly trimmed. The photographer organized us in two rows, according to age. Mom and Dad sat together holding baby Lonny and toddler Stephen. Cheryl and Tim sat beside me in the front, and Terry, Douglas, Linda, and Tom stood in the back. This was the only photo ever taken of my family. Soon after this day, my life on the farm would be over.

One morning, my mother came home with new shiny black shoes for my sister and me. Holding our new shoes in our laps, we went for an hour-long ride in the car to a place I knew would be filled with fun. We arrived at an enormous mansion with a ten-foot statue of a man with a long beard and a robe draped down to his bare feet. His hands were stretched out to the sky. With excitement I turned to the playground on the side, where a large crowd of children were playing near the biggest swing-set I had ever seen. As my mother let us go, we ran to the wooden swings and hopped on. It took a long time to get up into the air, but once I did, I remembered the wonderful feeling of freedom. I tried to touch the sky with my feet. I started to sing a song quite loudly.

As I looked up to find my mother, I saw her drive away. I was not worried or afraid. My seven-year-old sister had followed me to the swings. She was also trying to touch the sky with her feet. I don't remember my mother saying goodbye or providing any explanation. I was six years old. I would remain at the orphanage for eight years, until I entered the ninth grade, and at that time I was moved to a foster home.

Sheila at four (second from left) and her family, 1958

RADIO OF LIFE

I. INTRODUCTION

I read and I listened to the radio a lot before entering the orphanage, so it's not surprising that these became my main survival tools while I was there. Books offered an escape, whereas with songs I made connections. The words often reminded me of people, places and things. This story of my life is an example of how song lyrics, woven into my memories, represent my thoughts and feelings. My story shows how a little transistor radio became my "Radio of Life."

II. FIRST LESSON: BE LIKE SPOCK

The first lesson I learned upon entering the orphanage was that...

> *...smiling faces sometimes don't tell the truth.*
> *They show no traces of the evil that lurks within.*

As Sister Julienne led me to my dormitory, I could see the signs:

> *Signs, everywhere a sign. Do this. Don't do that.*
> *Can't you read the signs?*

In my imagination I saw another sign, one that read, "Do Not Feel." In order to survive, I needed to be like Spock from Star Trek. I needed to cut myself off from my emotions.

> *Any smile on my face is only there*
> *trying to fool the public.*
> *Really, I'm sad. I'm sadder than sad.*
> *And I'm hurting so bad.*

MAN IN THE MOON

Waking up to the screams of children: little girls being literally dragged out of bed from their slumber and beaten by two nuns was traumatic and terrifying. I never let myself fall asleep until I was certain the nuns had already gone to bed. One night I snuck into the bathroom and wrote this poem, to the Man in the Moon:

Shine on Man in the Moon for your light will
shine and never cease.
Your world is lonely, cold and barren
yet you have learned to cope.
You get to watch over everyone here on earth

without being a part of us
and without knowing the feelings of being alive.
Help me Man in the Moon. Please help me.
Help me to be like you are.

To just watch but not know or feel
what is happening.

IV. ALL THE SORROWS...

...sad tomorrows, take me back to my own home.
The world is a bad place, a sad place, a terrible
place to live,
but I don't want to die.
Until I did.

A long, long time ago I can still remember
how the music used to make me smile.
I knew if I had my chance...

I was being accused of planning to run away again. I'd been staying by myself to keep anyone else from getting in trouble. When Rosie and Amy asked to listen to my radio, I thought they would be safe because they were only 11. I was wrong. I knew then that because of me, they would be hurt by the nuns.

...something touched me deep inside and I knew
this will be the day that I die...

These were the last lyrics I heard before I cut my wrist.

V. ON A WINTER'S DAY

I was placed on the adult psychiatric ward of the hospital, where for the first month I'd...

> *...sit alone gazing from my window*
> *to the street below...*
> *...as I listened to my radio.*
> *I've built walls, a fortress deep and mighty*
> *that none may penetrate.*

Libby, one of the nurses, said that I reminded her of the song "I Am a Rock."

> *I have my books and my poetry to protect me.*
> *Hiding in my room,*
> *I touch no one and no one touches me...*

...until Linda, one of the nurses, who was hugging the one other girl on the ward while I was nearby, thought to hug me too. My family had not been affectionate, so I only knew to stand there like a wooden log as she threw her arms around me. She asked me if I knew how to hug. When I didn't answer, she took my arms and placed them around her waist. From then on, the nurses gave me hugs and even tucked me into bed at night.

I'd been warned by the nuns not to talk, so I could not say...

> *...Doctor my eyes have seen the years*
> *and a slow parade of fears without crying.*
> *Now I want to understand. I saw the evil.*
> *Where's the good? Help me if you can.*

Unfortunately, I was not helped while on the ward, other than learning what it was like to receive affection. I never returned to the orphanage. Because of my psychiatric hospitalization, I was deemed "not foster home material." The state had to find a place for me to go. That place was The Elizabeth Lund Home for Unwed Mothers (E.L.H.)

VII. A GOOD KID

E.L.H. staff were instructed by my social worker not to give me attention. Her concern was that by engaging with me, they would worsen my struggles with self-harm and suicidal thoughts. So, again, I did everything alone. I got up to the radio playing the Lone Ranger's "William Tell Overture." I went to school, did homework, chores, laundry, and kept my room clean. When I sprained my ankle and was on crutches, I threw the pillows I was using to elevate my leg down the stairs from the second floor to the basement. I had no idea, when it came time to go to bed, how to get everything back up. A group supervisor came into the basement. I asked her if I could ride up in the elevator. I was deeply hurt when she said no. I had no one to...

> ...give me love, give me hope nor help me cope.
> If I was loved would I grow?
> Would I blossom,
> would life flow?
>
> In the sun, the rain, the snow,
> if love is lovely,
> will I ever know?
> Seeds are planted, nourished and helped
> to grow.
> What about a child?

VIII. STILL STANDING

I always seemed to lose what I thought was mine...
...including my name.

Sometimes I saw my life just falling apart and all the rejection tearing at my heart. But deep inside hope was still alive.

Now I feel...
...it's really great for me to be here...

...working together with all of you. We've become a team, a force, working to hold accountable those who caused us harm. Every time we share our stories, we tell the stories of hundreds of other children. When we achieve justice for ourselves, we will have achieved justice for them as well.

AN INTRODUCTION

From 1964 through 1965, my siblings and I lived at St. Joseph's Orphanage on North Avenue in Burlington, Vermont. On September 10, 2018, Vermont Attorney General T. J. Donovan announced the creation of a task force to investigate claims of physical abuse, sexual abuse, and yes, even murder, at the former orphanage.

I was one of the children who was sexually and physically abused at St. Joseph's. I've carried the emotional scars of those horrible experiences with me all my life. For decades, I've kept silent about the embarrassing details of my abuse. However, with the report from the Vermont Attorney General's office due to come out, I hope my truths will no longer have to stand alone. With this report, the wrongdoing, on a massive scale, at the hands of nuns and priests, will no longer be so easily denied.

For many years, I've gone from therapist to therapist. None of this did much good. That was until I met my last therapist. She knew that I was a singer/songwriter, and she suggested that I write about my experiences in song form.

As a child I was very religious; I loved singing in God's name. But the abuses I endured at St. Joseph's made me lose all faith in God. I've tried over the years to regain that faith, but it seems it's lost forever.

One of my songs describes the very moment I remember losing the last piece of my faith. Another has helped me in a battle I've fought for over 50 years. Every single day, the refrain, "I don't want to do this! I don't want to do this!" has played over and over in my mind. Writing about the events where that refrain began, in lyric form, has shown me that my songwriting is a process that is both artistic and therapeutic. It helps me to reclaim, in some way, aspects of myself that I have lost. I recently produced a video (available on my Facebook page) to share several of my songs.

I DON'T WANT TO DO THIS

It happened a long time ago
But it still bothers him so.
It happened every Friday night
And the food was a frightening sight.

"I don't want to do this,
I don't want to do this."
He cried, oh, so…many times
For surely this, this must be a crime.

"Please, Please, don't make me do this."
Blood sausage is what they called it.
The very smell would made him sick.

It was dark red, and full of blood.
"Clean off your plate," she said.
"You don't need taste buds."

"I don't want to do this,
I don't want to do this."
He cried, oh, so…many times
For surely, this, this must be a crime.
"Please, Please, don't make me do this."

When he couldn't eat it, he got a paddle to the head.
He faced Friday nights with so much dread.
He choked it down, and it came right back up.
Then, forced to his knees to eat what he just threw up.

"I don't want to do this,
I don't want to do this."
He cried, oh, so…many times
For surely, this must be a crime.

"Please, Please, don't make me do this.
Please, Please, don't make me do this."

BETRAYED FAITH

He didn't know what was going on.
All he knew, it was oh...so wrong.
Covered his eyes, when she dropped to her knees,
As she took him, just as she pleased.

She betrayed her faith, destroyed his as well.
But he didn't know who he could tell.
Would anyone believe that betrayal he was dealt?
For he lost all...his faith, that day as she knelt.

Swallowed up by her veil, his faith so betrayed.
His innocence lost, his childhood delayed.
His faith in God went up in a flame.
For how could he let her do this in His name?

She betrayed her faith, and destroyed his as well.
But he didn't know who he could tell.
Would anyone believe that betrayal he was dealt?
For he lost all...his faith, that day as she knelt.

He said, "Please, I am clean."
She said, "No, you need more scrubbing."
Those days in the shower,
Were more than just troubling.
So, he covered his eyes, and let her have her way,
It still haunts him to this very day.

She betrayed her faith and destroyed his as well.
But he didn't know who he could tell.
Would anyone believe that betrayal he was dealt?
For he lost all...his Faith, that day as she knelt.

IN GOD'S NAME

As a child he loved God and his church,
And he loved singing in God's name.
But times were about to change,
From a loving home, to a place of shame.

It was called Saint Joseph's,
But far from a saintly place.
Where fear and terror
Were part of their daily disgrace.

He became an altar boy, just trying to fit in,
But filled with fear by that man's devilish grin.

"I don't want my mass held up,
So just pee and just shut up."
"But Father, I can do it by myself."

"No...young boys have really bad aim.
Do you really want to feel that shame?

Because, you know it's true,
I'll just hold it for you.

And so you won't feel that shame,
Just let the hand of God guide your aim."

He'd pee as fast as he could,
As his knees shook, right where he stood.
And when he was finally done,
He got a little rub on his bum.

Because of the father's hands-on,
His love for God was now gone.
Because of the fear and the shame,
He could no longer sing In God's name.

ORPHAN

In my life I have survived many types of traumatic experiences. The worst of these occurred at St. Joseph's Orphanage. I suffered physical and sexual abuse there, at the hands of those one should be able to trust the most.

My first memory of the orphanage was when we were surrendered. I watched my sister being marched to another wing. My brother and I held one another's hands. We were told to follow the nun to the boys' dormitory on the other side of the building. We were each given a number, along with a pillow, sheet, and blanket. My number was 25. I was placed on the little boys' side. My brother was number 35 and he was placed on the big boys' side. So we were all separated from one other and alone. That was when I learned how to fear.

The Sisters of Providence, who ordered us around, mostly came from poor and uneducated homes in Canada. They had no special training. From many of them, the best you could hope for was casual indifference. The rest were as mean as a nest of vipers. The breaking of the simplest of rules meant punishment. They liked their little tortures.

Have you ever been made to kneel with a hard bean under each knee? It's not as much fun as it sounds. Five minutes feels like a lifetime. Fifteen minutes later and you don't think you'll ever be able to walk again. Another little pleasantry they enjoyed was forcing you to stand, holding your arms straight out from your sides, with a heavy book in each hand. A nun would eye her pocket-watch. You didn't want to drop the books before the time ran out. If you did, you'd get hit on the back with a blackboard pointer.

27

You could receive these punishments for as little as failing bunk inspection, running on the stairs, or whispering in church. That was a biggie. Before St. Joseph's, I'd never been to church. So I hadn't known that whispering was against the rules. The nuns were not only creative with their tortures, but with what they deemed a punishable offense. I lived, therefore, in a constant state of fear.

By the time I left the orphanage, my number had been changed to five. I never let the numbers they assigned me define who I am. I think somewhere in their minds that was their intention. To take the only thing we had left: our sense of self, our willpower. But I refused to surrender.

THE CHILI CONTEST

As I was shopping for groceries one morning, I saw a flyer advertising a chili cook-off. Well, I said to myself, I make a good bowl of red chili; why not give it a try, see how it goes?! So I filled out an entrance form and got a copy of the rule book to study.

The rules were fairly straightforward: cook your best pot of chili using proper sanitation procedures, and have it judged accordingly. What's so hard about that? There were four prizes: you could win, place, or show.

The night before the chili contest I gathered my Coleman stove, my awning, and all my spices and peppers as well as my secret ingredient! You know all recipes need a secret ingredient. The contest started at ten o'clock; I was ready and set up by nine.

When the whistle was blown to start the contest, I immediately began searing off my cubed tri-tip and hamburger mix with a little olive oil on the bottom of my stock pot. Once that was seared off, I added a couple quarts of beef stock and let it simmer until the beef was tender. The sun beating down on my awning added to the heat from my stove on my face was almost too much, but I came to put up a good showing and that's what I was going to do.

I added the remaining ingredients, including my secret ingredient, and just let the chili meld together. It was a beautiful thing! The aroma wafting off of the pot was indescribable. Finally, time was called, and the sponsors sent people to pick up bowls of chili for each of the judges.

The sponsors also sold individual tickets. One of these got you a bowl of chili from a booth of your choice. The more tickets I received, the more votes I got. I was doing well; I was out of chili before they called time. As they announced the winners, I kept hoping to hear my name.

Third Place? Nope.
Second Place? Nope.
First Place? No.
Oh well. It's been an amazing day.
Wait, what's that? People's Choice Award!
They called my name. That's enough to keep me going.

I still do chili cook-offs from time to time, but let's save some stories for another day. I will reveal to you my secret ingredient, though: unsweetened baker's chocolate!

Debi Gevry-Ellsworth

THE THOUGHT OF YOU:
A REMEMBRANCE OF RONALD PAUL GEVRY

To Debbie Summer of
Love Ron 1985
LAKe Congamond
MASS

Ronald Paul Gevry (a.k.a. Ronnie) was born on November 2, 1961. At the age of three, he was placed, along with me and our sister, Cheri, at St. Joseph's Orphanage.
He was to remain there for ten years.

Ronnie's life started out hard, with severe abuse inflicted at the hands of our mother. When he entered the orphanage, he was a frightened toddler. He needed love, hope, and kindness, and what he received there was just the opposite. It was easy to see the progression of my brother's pain and rage. Each year we were at St. Joseph's it grew.

Ronnie tried his hardest to make the best out of life.
He was a good student and an excellent athlete. In the right circumstances and with gentle guidance he may have become a good man with morals and values, but that was not to be. Six months after we obtained our freedom from the hellhole of St. Joseph's, Ronnie was placed in a boys' juvenile detention center.

If you followed the slits on his arms you would get an idea of the suffering that he held inside. Cuts so close together they resembled burn marks rather than razor slits. When I was a child, it was hard for me to fathom why he cut and lied and stole and chased me around with bad intent, but I understand now. He lived what he learned.

When Ronnie was 18, he met a girl. She was wonderful and seemed to be just what he needed. They married and had a daughter. It did not take long for his wife to realize she had made a huge mistake, when Ronnie went to jail for the hundredth time. After he was released, he went home to his family. They tried hard to make it work, and in between tries a son was born. The boy was named Ronnie Jr.

After the last separation from his wife, Ronnie drifted from place to place, not knowing where to land. He tried to convince me to allow him into my house. But at this point I had a young daughter to protect. There was no way that my brother was going to get near her. He drifted off to California and that was the last I heard from him until the coroner called. My brother passed away at the age of 34, in some halfway house in God knows where, California. I didn't believe the coroner until he described the cuts down Ronnie's arms. At that point there was no denying it was him. My heart broke and I cried for days.

Ronnie was a victim in the purest sense. He sustained abuse at the hands of my mother, the nuns, the priests, and a system that was there to protect children. Today, I have forgiven my brother for the pain he redirected towards me. But I will never forgive the nuns and priests who inflicted so much abuse upon him that he broke. In the end, Ronnie was just an empty shell, living in his own hell. May the Lord hold him forever in his arms and may my brother rest in peace.

Cheri, Ronnie, & Debi, ten, seven & six, respectively

CROWBAR

Crowbar Crowbar
come pry this out
there's something in my gut
and I need help
so many methods I've tried in despair
chatted with many who pretended to care

I've sat for hours
with my fingers just right
I've prayed to God
well into the night
yet still it's stuck
this feeling I've got
that I'm just not right
I'm just not right

Crowbar Crowbar
you're iron strong
with your strength I can't go wrong
I am useless in this fight
weak and trembling I have no might

Crowbar Crowbar
use your steel
dig into the dirt
expose how I feel
each day is a struggle

the demons hover near
stealing from my life all that I hold dear

Crowbar Crowbar
forget what I say
I will seek a different way
because I know
as I grow old
that each day is a day I can be free
if I drop the rocks they loaded on me

THIS SISTER THIS SNAKE

Perched upon a wooden pew
well within my little view
sat a snake
tongue lashing its warning
eyes scanning
narrow pupils quickly moving
to-and-fro.

Draped in black and white
she kept her prey within her sight
and waited, spring loaded.
When would she strike?

I peered around the corner
just to have another look.
That's when I heard the rattle.
That's when my body shook.

Poisonous venom
ruptured my skin
millions of tears I held deep within
but the snake, she grinned
joyously recording another win

slithered back, a neat little ball
as if she'd never struck at all.
But I felt the pain.
It has yet to wane.

Jesus, Jesus on the wall
please save me
from this evil woman
who heard your call.

The cross that hung on a collared neck
the one that swung with every step
did it not remind her
of her choice
to walk with the Lord
to be his voice?

Still her French tongue thrashed
and her heavy hand bashed
until I came to believe
I was evil
I was mean.

In the darkness of those days
she tried her hardest
to have her way
to break me down, body and soul
to make me half not whole.

Instead I chose to seek the light
to find life's pleasures and its delights.
I smile when I want to cry.
I pray to the Lord with all my might.

I thank him every day
that I did not crumble
I did not break
beneath the sinister hand of
this sister
this snake.

MYSTERY OF THE HUMAN BEING

The artist is distinguished from all other responsible actors in society - the politicians, legislators, educators, and scientists - by the fact that he is in his own test tube, his own laboratory, working according to very rigorous rules, however unstated these may be, and cannot allow any consideration to supersede his responsibility to reveal all that he can possibly discover concerning the mystery of the human being.

— James Baldwin, The Creative Process

This is the day that the Lord has made. Let us be glad and rejoice in it.

The birds feel no need to recite these verses, for upon the branches they sit and sing to the early morning sun as the dew evaporates from the grass. The world goes around in such a regular way. Each day seems to duplicate the next, but in the tiny details, things change. From tiny they become big, huge even, and not a notice is taken until it is just too plain to see.

Do the birds notice their aging as they fly from tree to fence post to nest? Do they distinguish one year from the next? Why has God saddled humans with the knowledge of existence? It's a wonder to watch nature and in turn to watch humans as they interact within it. Why the anger, the sadness, the need to constantly be at odds with one another and the natural world? Did God not place peace into the heart of man? It is so easy to conjure up feelings of envy, hatred, and wishes for revenge. Yet, how far we must dig to find contentment, kindness, and understanding for our fellow man.

Sacred temples and ancient cathedrals seem to hold the blessing in a bubble. As if every human being that ever laid a brick, painted a wall, placed a candle, or held another's hand in prayer had added a special kind of oxygen. An atmosphere in which the next visitor could breathe and find peace. Could the entire earth be a temple?

ON REVISION: A CONVERSATION ABOUT PROCESS

Q: Can you talk a little bit about the process of developing and revising "This Sister, This Snake?"

A: I liked the way this grew through nine revisions. One of the things we learned was that we should save every draft. And I found that very useful. I would have a new idea or find a new direction. Then I'd read through my previous drafts. The first draft was very tight.

Q: I remember your saying that the draft was taut. I found that quality a powerful one in relation to the occasion of the poem. Can you describe what you mean by the poem being very tight?

A: There were sections I could expand, and I'd work with one section at a time, changing a couple of words here and there. That became the second draft. It was almost like hopscotch.

Q: An interesting image for the revision process! I notice that you changed the end a lot.

A: When I got to the end, I was having a problem with how hurried it felt. I realized I'd rushed through rather than diving into it. So I talked to my husband, and he said, "Why don't you make it a victorious ending…leave the poem on a high?" I sat with what he'd said for a while, two days. Then I just kept making more and more and more revisions. The process was amazing. Like when you write a story and you don't know where the characters came from. It's as if they've come out of the air. I knew the ending had to be victorious, that it somehow had to say, "I'm not going to let them win." It was cool to watch. Like watching a flower.

40

THE ROCK PAINTING & INSCRIPTION

Rock Painting, Katelin Hoffman

ROCK INSCRIPTION

In God's world, everyone has a place and is valued. Children were not meant to be hurt, regardless of whether they have families to love and protect them. I wish that the Sisters of Providence and Catholic Charities had known this. Maybe some of the pain and suffering that occurred so needlessly and senselessly wouldn't have happened. What child can understand the value of her own life when those who claim to represent God hurt her so viciously, sometimes when she hasn't even broken a rule. How can nuns and priests taunt innocent children with such intensity and to such an extreme that they take away those children's dignity, self-esteem, and perhaps even their desire to continue to live? To whom could those children turn if the only adults in their lives acted as if it were God's will that they be raped, molested, beaten, and humiliated? This is the story of the lives of the children at St. Joseph's Orphanage.

THE ROCK PROJECT, TALKING ABOUT THE INTERPLAY OF WRITING & VISUAL ART

Q: How did the rock paintings and inscriptions come about?

A: I did the writing first. I believe it was in 1996. Former children of St. Joseph's Debbie, Dane, and Donna Cote went for a tour of the orphanage. As they walked out behind the building to where the beach was, they spotted a seven-foot marble slab. Donna took out a magic marker and at the very top she wrote down their names and the numbers they'd been assigned while in the orphanage. She also wrote *In God We Trusted*. This was thirty years later for them, and twenty-four for me. Debbie asked if I could write something on the rock as well. So one day I visited the site and walked down to the rock to see what they'd written. Underneath their words, I started writing. I also had only a magic marker at the time.

Q: You've said you have a lot of photos of the rock in various stages of your artwork. How did your documentation of the project begin?

A: I took a picture of what I'd written so that I could show it to Debbie. She really liked it, and she said it should be the prologue of the book she wanted me to write. Later that summer, I returned to the rock. It was a private beach, all quiet, so, I thought, Well, how about I draw a picture of the orphanage and a few figures - of Debbie, Dane, and Donna?

Q: It's so moving and inspiring to hear about your process. How did the other images come to life?

A: I also painted a picture of the orphanage. Then I made a tiny self-portrait at the end of the first piece. I kept going back. I added the poem and the picture of an angel...I stuck the kids below the angel.... Finally, I decided to paint the whole rock. At the end of the angel poem, I painted a tiny figure of myself after I tried to kill myself.

Q: What did it feel like to paint that?

A: It was empowering. Because it was my truth. It sums it all up.

THE WRITER'S NOTEBOOK AS A TOOL
FOR GENERATING MATERIAL

Think of your writer's notebook as a place where you can collect all different types of writing.
Some examples:

- pieces of writing by writers whom you admire and whose writing inspires you
- dreams
- letters you will never send
- ideas
- hopes
- ticket stubs from movies, train rides, etc.
- photographs
- sketches
- observations
- journal entries

Your writer's notebook is a kind of living reminder that your work can take many forms. It is a kind of container where you can collect:

- fragments of writing of any size
- writing that may (or may not) be seeds, starting places, for larger pieces you can develop

AN EXPERIMENT:
MOMENTS/MEMORY FRAGMENTS
PART ONE:

Put on some music you love, preferably instrumental.
Make a list of short memories, whatever comes to mind:

- joyous
- difficult
- recent (including yesterday or this morning!)
- from a few years ago, many, anywhere in between
- Short is the operative word: a moment, an afternoon, a breakfast, walking your dog, etc.
- Try not to think too hard or dwell on any one aspect of your life. Just see what comes to mind. Allow yourself to be surprised.
- Write without stopping, preferably longhand. Just short descriptions, a few words, for each memory.

PART TWO:

Once you've collected some memories, anywhere from five or to six or more, look over what you've got, and work on what we'll call memory fragments:

- These fragments can be of any length: a few words, a sentence, a paragraph.
- The idea of this experiment is that down the line these may (or may not) be developed.
- It's best to aim here not to create a perfect piece of writing; you are simply collecting memories.
- The beauty of this exercise is that it allows you to linger on a single moment and bring it to life.

COLLABORATIVE CALL & RESPONSE WRITING EXPERIMENT

Our aim in this experiment was to use a call and response as a way into generating some writing. This can be an energy-filled way to begin to look at revision and editing. By cutting the "call" sections of the call and response, we were able to think about non-essential and essential parts of the first draft, which was spoken. And then to craft that spoken word into writing.

DRAFT I/PART I/SPOKEN

C: With my writing I would like to...
R: ...bring attention to the issues that we're working with...I think the biggest issue is that people don't believe...It's just too hard for people to believe...instead of "our story" ...we should call this "our truths."
C: With my writing I would like to...
R: ...express my desires and feelings about things that are important to me...such as coming to terms with my past.
C: With my writing I would like to...
R: ...heal my wounded heart.
C: With my writing I would like to...
R: ...help my children to understand who I am and who I was and why I am the way I am.
C: With my writing I would like to...
R: ...help people not only envision but also feel what it was like to be at the orphanage.

PART II: SPOKEN

C: With my writing I have already begun to…
R: …heal.
C: With my writing I have already begun to…
R: …learn so much about myself.
C: With my writing I have already begun to…
R: …realize how deep the damage is done.
C: With my writing I have already begun to…
R: …understand who I am and accept my idiosyncrasies.

DRAFT II:
CUTTING NON-ESSENTIAL WORDS,
BRINGING OUT WHAT IS ESSENTIAL

OUR WRITING
to bring attention to the issues that we're working with
to express our desires and feelings about what's important
to us
to come to terms with the past
to heal our wounded hearts
to give our children an understanding
of who we are and who we were
and why we are the way we are
to help people not only envision
but also feel
what it was like to be at the orphanage

BEGINNING
I have already begun to heal.
I have learned so much about myself.
I have realized how deep the damage is that has been done.
I have come to accept my idiosyncrasies.
I have come to understand who I am.

TWO: ONE YEAR LATER

The question was a seed, planted into the soul of anyone who cared to walk this path of healing. And so we nourished that seed with our words and our memories. Oh, the pain and the joy of words, our words.

Together we grew, becoming seedlings, sometimes bending in the spring breeze, sometimes stretching towards the sun. Each sentence placed on a page, each song, story, or poem written strengthening our roots until we became stronger, more grounded.

Just as an acorn grows into a towering oak tree, so have we grown, this group of writers who once experienced a living hell, simply by being brave enough to write our truths no matter the cost.

— Debi Gevry-Ellsworth

Debi Gevy-Ellsworth

BRICKS AND MORTAR

If bricks were scales and mortar
flames
this monstrosity of a building
would be a dragon
burning children that wear no cross

High upon a hill
the beast sprawls
stretching four story wings
to the north and to the south

Slated head
crowned with golden crucifix
punctures the Vermont sky
screaming religion

Colossal single pane eyes
scan the Green Mountains
for sins for lies

Damaged parents with their damaged offspring
stumble forward
unaware of the deception
unaware of the disguise

Climbing the spotless marble steps
the ragged enter
and take their rest

the front parlor hides true intent
with statues and tapestries and
paintings of saints and martyrs and Christ
visitors are washed in the false peace
one feels
when gazing upon eternal life

Behind solid oak doors
lies a maze of dark hallways
that lead only to the chapel
or the boiler room
where the fire hides
waiting
Upon entering
children are lost wandering
in millions of red bricks
their innocence
immediately incinerated

If their laughter
their energy
could vibrate the walls
pierce the heart and
escape into the universe
perhaps life would be better for all
But the windows are painted shut
and mouths muted

ONCE

on chords recognized long ago
now forgotten
in the year I realized
I am old

the mirror told me so
once I looked so close
I nearly left traces

and you
gone
scattered to the wind
in a lake up north

shards of gray rode on
tips of white caps
seeking sandy shores

we are all
earthbound in the end
once our bones were young
pliable willing
we danced
the aisles of stadiums
civic centers opera houses
and once just once
spectacular Red Rocks

you my Tin Man
pulsated with the beat of the drums
me your Willow
swayed in the breeze of Jerry's notes

once we joined
60,000 voices
we sang beneath the evening sky
a celestial cathedral
a stoned out choir

spirit they say
is always there
on the wind
on the notes
in a song

are you still dancing
singing can you
when your bones are dust

GURU TOO

bought a book
actually read it
the author a well-known guru
who right now as i write this
is dying in the PRESENT
allowing the pain
inviting the fear

will he transcend SELF
reach NIRVANA
i know not
his state of MIND
yet i wonder
is he free from EGO
as i cling to mine
amazing the methods i seek
to untangle the threads of my life
i am a cat in yarn
a fish in a net
a mouse in a trap
snap
the guru says pain is all in thought
all in the need to be anywhere
but in the NOW
does that even make sense
artists see the world
on a slant
they are sort-of-gurus
with an eye for soft hues and dark nights
once i attempted to look at a tree
like an artist an intelligentsia
but it just looked like a red maple
i got discouraged and went scurrying back to my book
to my guru
i need answers
why do my eyes adjust to pain and pain alone

MY SWEET ROSIE

Out of the hundred photos I have lying around I chose you.

I chose you because I miss you.

I miss you with all my being.

You, with feeble legs that no longer run,

you, with eyes that no longer see,

you, with ears that no longer hear...

I was your sheep, and you my shepherd.

You never abandon your post.

My faithful friend to the end,

your eyes never left mine even when

the needle entered your right leg.

You sighed and it was up to me to close your beautiful eyes.

A LETTER

Dear Rosie,

It has been four months since I have last seen your graying face, last looked into your cloudy eyes. I think of you every day and I wish you were still here by my side, watching me. A dog's life always seems too short.

I remember the day you arrived, flying into New England from Arkansas. You were a shivering little red and white fuzz ball. I lifted you from the shipping crate and held you close. All the way home I snuggled you and whispered *Rose* into your tiny ears. Rose was the name Levi gave you when he was just nine years old. A perfect name for a perfect pup.

I had never raised or trained a border collie before, and I was hoping I was up to the task, as border collies are a herding breed and need to be worked. So you and I worked together and training you, my sweet Rose, was a breeze. We learned tricks, many, many tricks. We played frisbee and even joined some competitions, but that wasn't for you, so we stuck to the tricks. Do you remember how much joy you gave the patients at the nursing home where we volunteered once a week? I do. It is forever embedded in my mind.

The thing I miss most about you, my Rosie, is your stare. Never did your eyes leave mine. I was your sheep and you were my shepherd. It could be unnerving at times, but I got used to your watchful eyes, and now I miss them so very much.

Seventeen and a half years goes by in a blink of an eye when you spend it with a best friend, and that you were. I need to tell you, Rose, that the hardest decision I have ever made in all my 58 years was walking you out onto the porch that cold winter morning. I know you thought we were going for our morning walk. You trusted me, and to be honest with you I didn't mean to break that trust, but it was time, and in my heart I know I was doing the right thing for you.

I didn't think I was strong enough but I just knew I could not let you go alone, so with all the strength I had I held you tight just like the day you came to me, and I spoke to you, whispered in your ear that all would be well. You looked up at me as that needle, that drug-filled, you're-never-coming-back needle, was placed into your right leg and within minutes you were gone, and it was up to me to close those beautiful, watchful eyes for the last time.

'Til we meet again, my Rosie

SPIRITUAL EVENTS

You've probably never heard anyone say this before, but cancer was the best thing that ever happened to me. Cancer was the best teacher I've ever had.

In 2005, within a period of six months, I went through 600 hours of chemotherapy. During that time, I experienced three spiritual events. Strangely enough, all three happened within the same week.

One morning, I was lifting weights in my basement. The chemo had drained me so badly that I had to work out early in the day while my energy was at its highest. I had just put down a set of weights, and I was leaning against the bench. All of a sudden, I was no longer in my body. I was way out in the universe somewhere. I couldn't see the earth or the moon. But what I could see were billions and billions of stars, like sparkling holes in a huge deep blue blanket. The depth of my vision was not three-dimensional, but more as if I was seeing six or seven dimensions. It was as if I could see around corners. The sharpness of my vision wasn't 20/20 but more like 0/0. I had never seen anything so crystal clear. The color saturation of the deep blue sky was mesmerizing. It literally took my breath away. I was totally aware of my consciousness as I was having a conversation with myself as to the beauty that was before me. The emotions that I felt were almost indescribable. Imagine what it would be like if all your problems were completely gone: no money problems, no health problems, no kid problems. Every negative situation in my life had vanished. That's what it felt like out there in the universe.

When I turned around to look for the earth and the moon, I realized I didn't have a body. I was pure energy. "Oh no," I thought. "Am I dead?" With that, I was immediately back in my body in our basement. I've tried for many years in many ways to return. I guess I'll have to wait until I die. This experience changed my life forever. I'm not in any hurry to die, but I no longer fear death itself.

The second event took place when my wife and I were on our way to work. We saw two deer in a field cut in half by a long dirt road. As we turned and drove down that road, we expected the deer to be long gone. Much to our surprise, they were still in the same place. I jumped out of the car, turned away from the deer and grabbed my binoculars, mistakenly slamming the door. I said to myself, "Oh god, they're definitely gone now!" But instead they were walking right towards me. About twenty feet to the right, two turkeys were strolling straight at me. "What in the world is going on here?" I thought. "These are wild animals!" Just as I looked back at my wife to see if she was seeing the same thing I was, two ducks flew over the top of my head and landed ten feet to my left, and just sat there staring at me.

"Geez, this is almost like Noah's ark," I thought. "Everyone in pairs, one of each!" A feeling of oneness with these animals flushed over me from head to toe. Why were they all drawn to me? Why did they not fear me? Until recently, I could not understand.

A few days later I was driving home from work. It was so dark I never saw the dog until he was right in the middle of my grill. I didn't even have time to even touch the brakes. We could hear his body being crushed under the car as our right rear tire ran over him, sliding the car a bit to the left. As I turned back around and drove towards him, my heart was breaking, for I thought I had just killed this beautiful animal.

But as we approached, we could hear him crying. I started crying myself. At that very second, he went quiet. I was afraid his silence meant that he had died.

When my wife and I got out of the car we saw the dog's owner standing over him. My wife, being the animal lover that she is, ran to him and quickly looked his body over from head to toe. I was worried that, as he'd been injured, he might bite her. But she never gave it a second thought. All she could find was a tiny nick on his nose, not even any blood. "What?" I thought. "How could this be?"

The three of us stood there with our jaws hanging down. How was this possible? Suddenly an idea flashed into my head. I was so brokenhearted at this moment that I thought perhaps my father sensed my pain. He had died three months before, and he had always been an avid dog lover. It occurred to me that maybe my father had a hand in this spiritual event. As soon as the dog was on the leash, he was in fact so strong and fit he literally dragged his owner across the street. Later, we would often see the dog being walked in town, and it was such a great relief to know I had not killed this beautiful animal.

If my wife had not witnessed these three moments, I would by now have blown them all off as a dream. But I know these mysterious happenings were real, and over the years, I've come to understand how they all came out of my experience with cancer. Before I began the chemo, I was told there was a 50/50 chance it could kill me. As I looked death in the face, my attitude towards life completely changed. I found myself suddenly more peaceful. I now believe that the animals in that field who normally would have feared a human were drawn to me because of the peaceful place I was in. While I am an atheist, I cannot deny or explain these three spiritual events. They will, however, remain my fondest memories.

Katelin Hoffman

SEEMS LIKE I LIVED A LIFETIME IN MY FIRST SIX YEARS

The world offers itself to your imagination,
calls to you like the wild geese, harsh and exciting –
over and over announcing your place
in the family of things.
— Mary Oliver

When I was a very young child, about two, my grandmother would sit with me at the kitchen table in the Quonset hut we rented, while we drank coffee and I listened to her stories about my family and the trouble created by my birth.

My crib was near the white-with-golden-specked Formica table. After my mother left for work, dropping my brother off at school, I would climb up into my highchair opposite my grandmother, ready to drink my coffee (mine was rather sweet and milky, of course) and go on her journeys.

I was the perfect audience, because I never talked. My grandmother spoke to me about anything and everything, as if I understood. And I think I did understand. I rarely spoke before I was three, as it felt safer to stay quiet. Even at two, I knew something was wrong with my mother. My grandmother helped me to understand my mother was ill and had been placed in a hospital not long after I was born. From the time I was two, I took responsibility for her mental troubles and for the family breakup, figuring it was my birth that had caused my mother's illness.

My mother told me that my father wasn't really my father, that she had different parents than my grandparents, that she had triplets named Tayton Tackle, Nathan Nackle, and Payton Packle. I knew her world did not match the one that others in my life lived in. But when she beat me with a belt for things my brother did, I thought I was being punished because of the problems caused by my birth.

61

Safe did not seem to be in my vocabulary. My grandmother was a backwoods Vermonter and thought nothing of allowing me to have complete access to the outside world. Both she and her twin sister had been placed at St. Joseph's Orphanage, and when she was ten, her sister died. I imagine that she must have felt trapped and alone as a child and that she wanted me to feel free. People did not like having toddlers wandering around wherever they wanted to go, but it worked for me!

I became a rather adventurous baby. There was a pear tree in the back yard. The pears would fall to the ground, drawing bees I would play with. I thought they were "baby bees." I learned the hard way that not all creatures like getting played with. One day, when the snake I'd picked up wanted me to know it did not want to play, it bit my arm, causing severe swelling. Now I was going to have to talk. I said, "A big bug bit me." I had to go to the hospital because no one knew what this "big bug" was.

In Poquonock, Connecticut, where we'd lived until I was three, there had been no place to roam and explore, but when we moved to Thompsonville, my world changed drastically. Here there were houses and streets and cherry trees that dropped sweet little red balls that tasted delicious. It was on one of my walks to a cherry tree that a woman came out of her house and asked me if I knew where I was. I thought she was angry with me for being near her house and ran away. It was only years later, when I thought about it again, that I realized I was only a three-year-old and this neighbor must have been concerned for my safety.

Nearly all children need help to learn certain things, such as how to ride a bike, roller skate, or ice skate. I never did. The first bike I rode was so big I couldn't even reach the seat. It's almost like God blessed me with certain abilities, things I could just do, as I had no one to teach me.

When I was only months old, I could walk and climb, perhaps becoming the youngest escape artist in history. It was my natural independence that one day led me to the bathroom like a cat to its litter box. The toilet in the Quonset hut was the same style as an outhouse, and too high for even the most determined two-year-old. Unused to asking for help, I did what came naturally. Standing on my brother's step stool, I reached up and put my two hands into the hole so that I could pull myself up. My grandmother, seeing where I was heading if I reached the top, managed to catch me. Apparently, the thought of fetching a toddler who'd tumbled down the toilet hole into a cesspool was unappealing. A lock too high for me to reach was placed onto the bathroom door.

When I was five, we were living in Windsor Locks, across the street from the Knights of Columbus, who employed a security guard for the sole purpose, it seemed, of keeping kids from setting up a rope to swing over a deep ravine. Once, my brother, Mike, a friend of his named Cecil, and I made it across with the guard right behind us. Since we could not swing back to go home, we followed Cecil through a swampy area by walking over a log. He said not to fall because we were crossing quicksand. I didn't believe it until a few years ago when I googled "quicksand in Connecticut." Cecil, it turns out, was telling the truth.

Looking back on those years with my grandmother, I am so appreciative of the freedom she allowed me and the ways she helped me to understand my mother's illness. I don't think I ever knew I was just a toddler, or a child who needed protection. Strangely, this helped me survive.

I only had a short time with my grandmother. She lived with us until I was five, and then my mother beat her and sent her away. Before leaving, my grandmother told me that someday someone would come and take my mother away. I now knew it would be my job to take care of my mother. At six I started first grade. My school was still practicing "duck and cover."

I thought of my mother, home and alone without me, being blown to bits. I needed to figure out a way to protect her. I did not know the crisis had ended, that we were no longer in immediate danger of being bombed.

I got up one Saturday morning with the idea of building a fallout shelter for my mother. I picked up the oldest spoon I could find, went out to the front yard, found a space I thought would be big enough, and started digging. The hole I dug was as long as I was tall and about ten inches deep by the time I finished. I knew I had a lot more digging to do. To me, it was going to be a real fallout shelter even though, as I had no supplies to fill it with, in reality what I'd dug would just remain an empty hole.

I had been determined, because of my mother's mental illness, not to use my imagination. But this was impossible. In fact, I was imagining all the time. I was solving problems in the ways that I could, using my creativity in order to survive. *The world offers itself to your imagination.* That hole was good enough after all!

FREEDOM BEHIND BARS

As a young adult, I had problems with authority figures.
The orphanage staff had raised me to have no other choice.
You had four kinds of staff. Some were there for a paycheck
only and had no care for children or for their concerns.
You had some who were very cop-like and authoritative.
There were some who treated children as if they were toys.
They were joyful and they laughed a lot, but this was always
at the expense of a child. They would incite the children to
bully one another. Finally, there were the young adults who
had gone through college with plans to go into social work.
They believed they had good places in their hearts for
children. Fresh out of school, they had lots of ideas on how
children should be raised. But those theories worked on
paper and not in person.

After my orphanage experiences I traded one form of
institutionalization for another by joining the navy. I enjoyed
the work and the traveling but, ultimately, because of the
way I'd been raised, I was not a good candidate for military
service. After three and a half years I was discharged for
swearing at a superior officer. I received an-other-than
honorable discharge. This was just a foretelling of what was
to come.

When I got out of the navy, I began using marijuana to self-
medicate, and to support this addiction I started to deal.
For about a year, I was making a living; I was under the radar.
Then a customer gave me the runaround over a thirty-dollar
bag of pot; he kept saying he'd pay me. This went on for
about a month. I finally managed to track him down. It was at
that moment that my life changed.

"Henry" was waiting for me as I sat down to order. While we
were eating, I asked him what was up about the money he
owed to me. He told me he had no intention of paying and
there was nothing I could do about it. I instantly felt a raw
heat and picked up my steak knife. I stabbed him in the side
of the neck.

65

He went into shock, ran out into the parking lot and collapsed. I went into instant disbelief. I hadn't known I was going to do it until I'd already done it. I waited, in shock myself, in the parking lot until the police arrived. They placed me in the back of the squad car. This was routine for them, just another day at the office. That night was the first night among many I would spend behind bars.

I was initially charged with attempted second-degree murder, then was offered a plea deal of aggravated assault. I took the deal. I was to serve four to ten years, with the four only if I stayed out of trouble and completed drug rehabilitation and anger management classes. Needless to say, I did not stay out of trouble or even start my mandatory programs. I even held the record, for a short time, for days spent in "the hole." I was of course denied parole after four years.

Being in prison, there is not much to do. There was reading, which I took complete advantage of, classes of all sorts, most of which I found to be uninteresting. I played a lot of cards. Sports and weightlifting were also available, so I did a lot of training as well. In that time, I had to learn on my own how to deal with my own anger. Mostly I did this through avoidance, keeping myself out of any situations in which I would be forced to be angry.

Five years into my sentence, I met a guard who was a practicing Buddhist. He was very self-possessed and quiet. He didn't make an issue of things. He would just let you know what you needed to do, and you would listen. For him, his job was not a power or control type of situation. He would discuss different Buddhist writers with very eclectic teaching styles such as D. T. Suzuki, Walpola Rahula, Thich Nhat Hanh, and Ajahn Chah, who is a particular favorite of mine.

The thing that struck me about him was how he embodied the Buddhist concept of right livelihood. I thought that being a prison guard made this concept questionable, but he made it an honorable profession.

This guard would talk to me about the four noble truths of Buddhism and help me understand them. These are: the truth of suffering, the truth of the cause of suffering, the truth of the end of suffering, and the truth of the path that leads us out of suffering.

He also taught me the Noble Eightfold Path: 1) Right View (all actions have consequences), 2) Right Intention (the intent to follow the path of the Buddha), 3) Right Speech (no lying, no rude speech, no gossip), 4) Right Conduct (no killing or injuring, no taking what is not given), 5) Right Livelihood (no unwholesome jobs), 6) Right Effort (working on clearing the mind of negative thought), 7) Right Mindfulness (being mindful of the teachings, not being absent-minded), and 8) Right Concentration (in meditation and all things).

I was intrigued; all of this got me thinking of how I wanted to live, which way I was headed, and if this was how I wanted to live my life: through a revolving prison door. I resolved to take drug rehabilitation and anger management classes and completed them. After I had been out of trouble and compliant, I was moved to a minimum-security facility and spent my last year there.

I wish I could remember his name. I'm sorry I can't. I guess I remembered the teachings though. He had a very stoic personality. He was a Marcus Aurelius kind of guy. He was very straightforward in everything he did. His kindness towards me was almost impersonal. You know how Buddhists are very neutral. He didn't play favorites, yet he spent time with me when he could have ignored me.

I do remember the moment it all became clear to me. I was walking back from the library and all of a sudden, a lightbulb flickered on in my head. That's when it dawned on me that there had to be a better way than the road I had taken. I resolved then and there to turn my life around, and that's what I did.

67

ABOUT THE WRITERS

GENE CLARK (1952)

Gene and his three siblings lived at St. Joseph's Orphanage from 1964 through 1965. They were raised by a single mother. "She made sure we felt love and kindness. Once we were placed at the orphanage our whole lives changed. We went from a loving home to a place of shame, with sexual and physical abuse being part of our daily lives. After having survived St Joseph's, I went on with my life, trying to fix all the damage that was done in that sinful place. My love for music seemed to be my only refuge."

Music also led to Gene's discovery of his talent for lyric-making and composing. "I found songwriting intensely healing and therapeutic." His love for music led him to build a recording studio. "I built Geno's Music Studio to ensure I'd be able to play tunes and write songs for the rest of my life. No one can ever take that away from me, for music is an important part of who I am. I now have the freedom to work in the studio whenever I want to, day or night. That's happiness!"

Gene lives with his wife Nancy in Essex Junction, Vermont. They have five children and fourteen grandchildren.

DEBI GEVRY-ELLSWORTH (1962)

Debi's love for writing and reading began early in life.
In fifth grade, she started keeping a diary and has yet to stop.
At the age of two, along with her sister and brother, Debi
was placed at St. Joseph's Orphanage. It would be ten years
before Debi re-entered society. "After I left the orphanage I
did not know how to live outside of an institution. I was like
a scared, feral cat, always watching my back, always ready to
run. There were three women who entered my life and each
of them, in their special way, showed me how to live. If not
for them, I haven't a clue where I'd be today. I am forever
grateful to them all. In high school I started writing poetry.
I knew nothing about sentence structure or composition;
I just enjoyed writing and it helped clear my mind.
Sometimes, if the opportunity arose, I would take a writers'
workshop, but for the most part I just wrote on my own until
we started the S.J.O.R.I. writers' group."

Today Debi lives on a 174-acre farm in Connecticut with her
husband, Jim, and their two dogs. They enjoy spending time
with their joined family of six children and five grandchildren.

SHEILA GRISARD (1955)

Sheila was born in Enosburg Falls, Vermont, the seventh of nine children. "My parents were poor and uneducated and went through many hardships. They were forced to place me and five of my siblings at St. Joseph's in 1961. In 1968, at the age of 14, I left the orphanage and was placed in three foster homes over a period of several years. One year later, I met a social worker who told me I could do whatever I wanted and live anywhere I liked as long as I did well in school. This motivated me to excel in academics, and I graduated one year early. I received a Tyrrell scholarship and attended Johnson State College, majoring in social work. I took a creative writing class in college and it was a lot of fun. This inspired me to keep journals, a practice I've continued throughout my life."

Sheila later attended nursing school and has worked for many years at the University of Utah Hospital. In 2001, she lost her partner in a skiing accident, an avalanche. "It was really from that time that I dove into humanitarian work. In 2014, I met my match, an orthotist who shares my passion for humanitarian work, and together we've traveled all over the world."

Sheila lives in Utah with her husband. They have two children and four grandchildren who also live in Utah. Sheila continues her work as a nurse. "But my real passion in life is my humanitarian work around the world. I have documented that part of my life in journals, detailing the cases we've worked on and writing about different cultures and people."

KATELIN HOFFMAN (1957)

Katelin wrote her first poem as a child, during her time at the orphanage, and throughout her life she's continued to write poetry. "In college, I wrote a lot of research papers, but I really never wrote my stories until later. I really enjoy writing personal narratives. It's kind of an exploration, where I get a sense of who I am and who I was, and how to relay that to other people. When I write about my experiences, it's a kind of therapy. I've learned through this work a lot about my emotions, and about what's important to me."

"I lived at the orphanage from 1970 to 1972, and then at the Elizabeth Lund home for three years. I was able to leave when I graduated early from high school. I've spent most of my life in and out of psychiatric hospitals. I've never married and never had a real home. But I've had five fur-baby children, three of whom are deceased."

Katelin studied social work at the University of Vermont for a little over three years. She finished her degree at Burlington College with a degree in psychology and human services.

"Ever since I was in third grade, I've admired Dr. Spock. I've tried to emulate him in his ability to not feel and to be logical. That's what makes the writing hard. But I love using my imagination in figuring out how to describe my past. Through this process, my goal is to make my experiences real for the reader."

Katelin lives in Burlington, Vermont, with a dachshund named Samantha Amber Rose and a cat named Oliver Liberty Blue. Sam is twelve and a half years old, and Oliver is three and a half.

MICHAEL RYAN (1964)

Michael entered St. Joseph's in 1973, at the age of nine, and he would remain at the orphanage for seven years. "I began reading at a very early age, kindergarten and even before. I would sit on my father's lap and he'd read to me, and that's how I learned. It has been an integral part of my life ever since." When Michael got out of the orphanage, he joined the navy. After the institutionalization of St. Joseph's and the abusive behaviors of authority figures there, he found that the military was "not a good fit."

"My travels have brought me from coast to coast, from the Mojave Desert to the infamous grapevines on the West Coast, to seeing the Statue of Liberty from the cab of my truck! I've been snow-blind in blizzards so heavy I could barely see the taillights of the truck in front of me, in fog so deep coming off Afton mountain in Virginia I could not continue.

"I was a commercial fisherman in Alaska. I sold flooring in Virginia, and I was a cross-country truck driver for many years. Wherever I was, you could always find me with a book in my hand. *The Prophet* is one of my favorites. Then, of course, there's *Sonnets From the Portuguese*. I've chosen these examples because they're both about love and the possibilities of love. I've always written a little bit here and there, but the S.J.O.R.I. writers' group is the first series of workshops I've ever taken. The only thing I enjoy more than writing is reading. I know how a story is supposed to go together, because I've read enough stories."

Michael lives with his wife, Laura, in Buckingham, Virginia. In his spare time, he likes to cook and compete in cook-offs. Chili is his specialty. He's been in the top five regionally on two separate occasions.

SPECIAL THANKS

I would like to thank my sweet wife for sticking by me all these years. I know that when we read our vows, we said, "in sickness and in health." But I think a lot of women would have left twenty surgeries ago. I'd also like to thank her for standing by my side as I've chased my music dream most of my life. I don't know what I did to deserve her, but I sure am glad she's mine.
— Gene Clark

I would like to thank God for His love. This is the one thing they couldn't steal. And anyone in my phone's contact list, consider yourself acknowledged as well.
— Debi Gevry-Ellsworth

Two people were very significant in my life and I would have gone another way if I hadn't met them. One was my high school friend, Fernando Perez. The other was Susan Smith, a social worker. I'd like to thank my children, Ashley Collins and Michael Cardwell, for continuing to encourage me to do the work I feel most passionately about.
— Sheila Grisard

There have been too many people in my life I'd like to thank to name them all. Most of all, I'd like to acknowledge those who've helped me along the way. At this time, I will express my appreciation to Misty, "Squeaks," Samantha, Oliver, and Molly. And a special appreciation to Carol Adinolfi, the St. Joseph's Orphanage advisory team, and The Voices of St. Joseph's.
— Katelin Hoffman

I would like to thank my beautiful wife who helped save me from myself, who inspires my writing with her support, and who makes me a better person every day!
— Michael Ryan

AN APPRECIATION

*Marc has given so much of himself for our healing.
When I first joined The Voices of St. Joseph's and we
talked, just the two of us, he asked 'If you could have
anything to help you heal, what would it be?' When
I told him that I wanted to start a writers' group, he
acted immediately. I think he's the first person in this
type of role who's ever truly listened and responded
so fully.*

— Debi Gevry-Ellsworth

The writers' group would like to thank Marc Wennberg for
his unwavering support. Without him, this process would not
have been possible. He has unselfishly given his time and
energy to all aspects of the inquiry throughout the past two
years. He has facilitated the forming of the writers' group
and brought our work forward by organizing many readings.
He has called us after every reading to check that we're
okay. In so many ways, he's gone beyond the call of duty. He
understands the importance of this anthology and has put
that understanding into action. We are deeply grateful for all
of his heartfelt efforts on our behalf.

— Gene Clark, Debi Gevry-Ellsworth, Sheila Grisard,
Katelin Hoffman, & Michael Ryan

CPSIA information can be obtained
at www.ICGtesting.com
Printed in the USA
BVHW030445140222
628897BV00006B/13